I SPY EWW GROSS!

© 2021 Webber Books

All rights reserved. This book or any portion thereof may not be reproduced or used in any manner whatsoever without the express written permission of the publisher except for the use of brief quotations in a book review.

Welcome to

I SPY

EWW GROSS!

GOOD LUCK!

I SPY with my little eye, something beginning with...

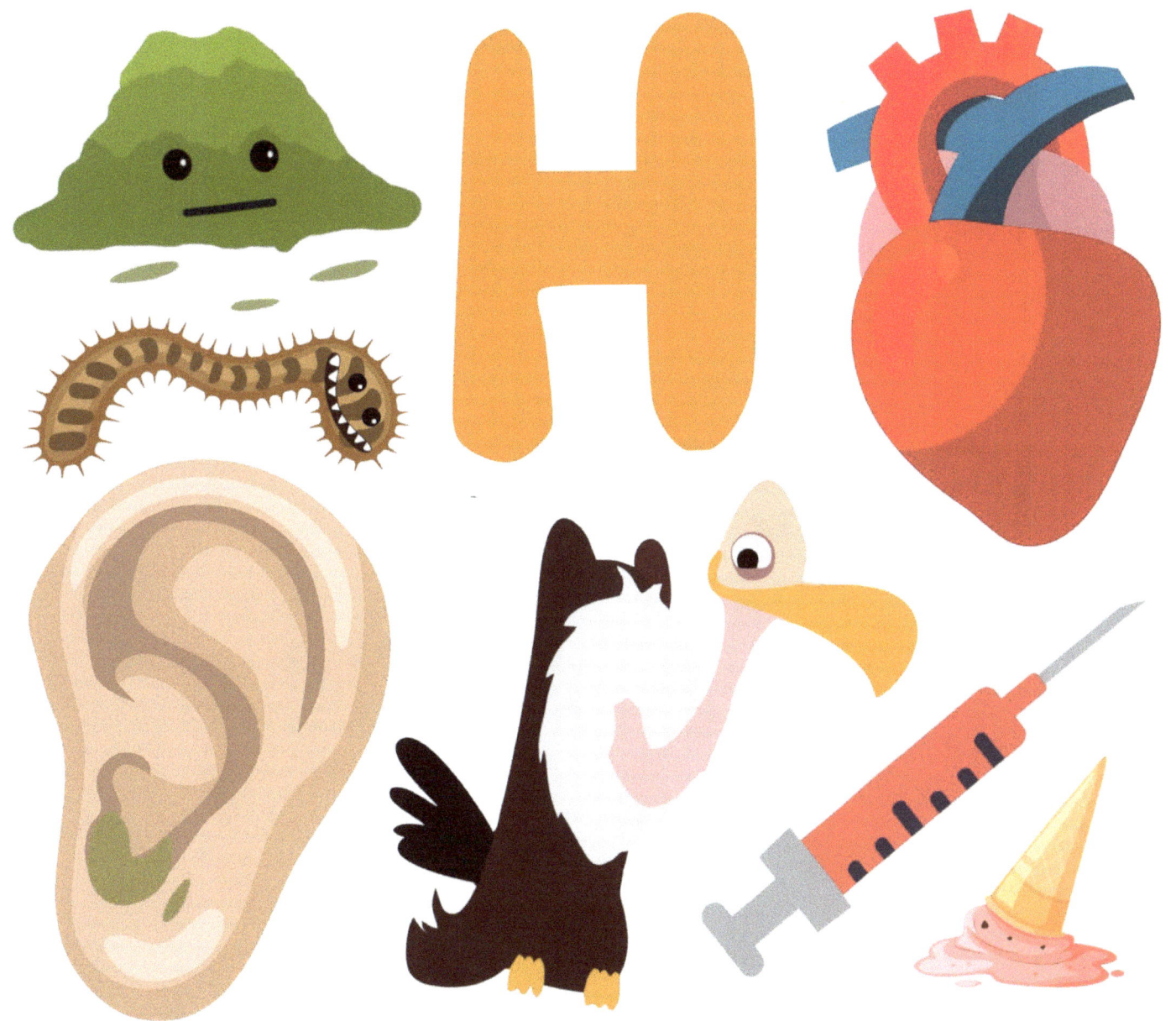

H is for HEART!

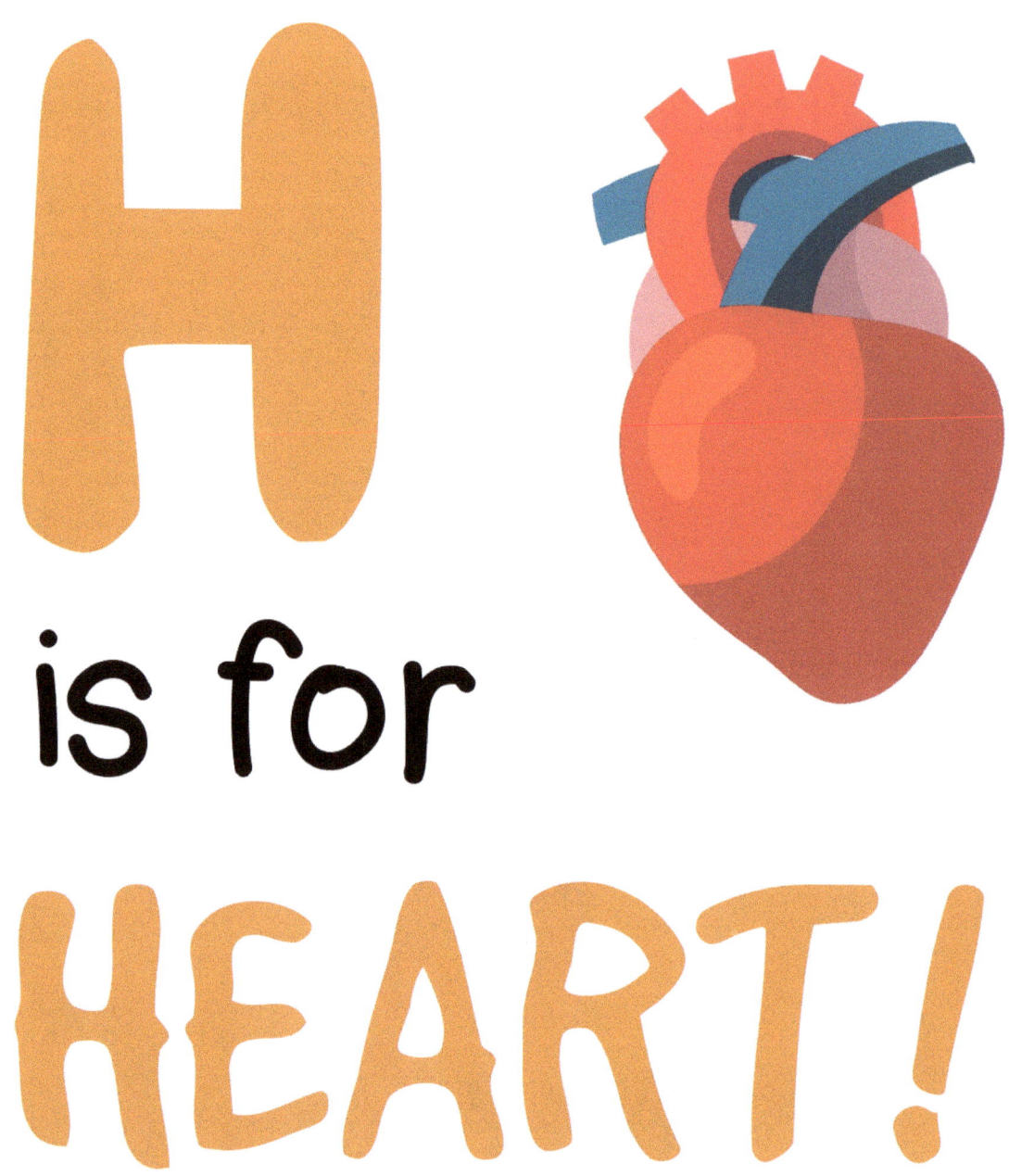

I SPY with my little eye, something beginning with...

D is for DIRTY DISHES!

I SPY with my little eye, something beginning with...

I SPY with my little eye, something beginning with...

I SPY with my little eye, something beginning with...

E is for

EYEBALL!

W
is for
WALRUS!

I SPY with my little eye, something beginning with...

B is for BACTERIA!

I SPY with my little eye, something beginning with... K

K

is for

KISSING!

I SPY with my little eye, something beginning with...

G is for GARLIC!

I SPY with my little eye, something beginning with...

C is for CHICKEN POX!

I SPY with my little eye, something beginning with...

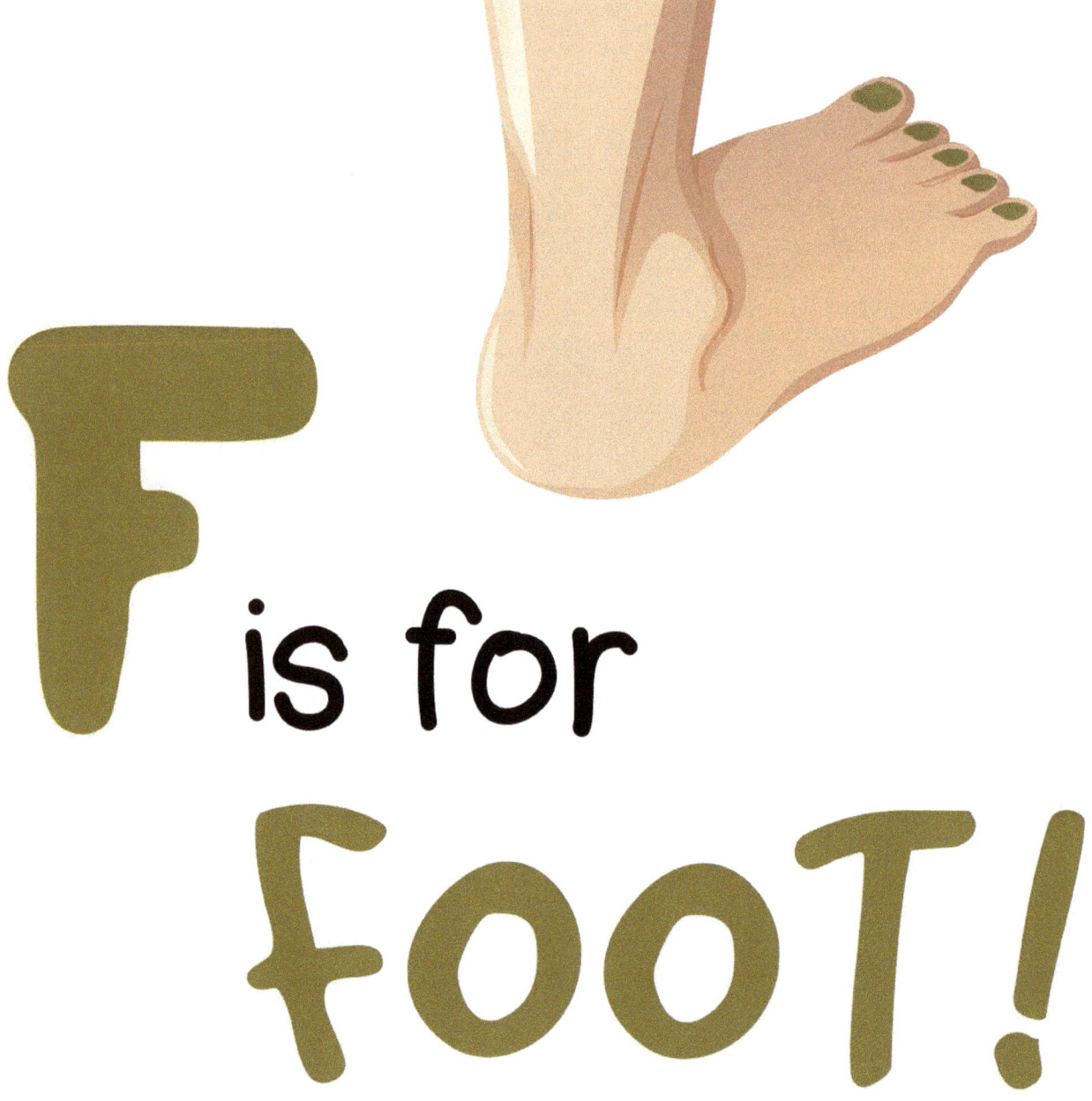

Z is for ZOMBIE!

I SPY with my little eye, something beginning with...

P is for Poop or Poo!

I SPY with my little eye, something beginning with...

V is for Voodoo Doll!

I SPY with my little eye, something beginning with...

S is for

SMELLY STINKY SOCK!

THE END!

Find us on Amazon!

Discover all of the titles available in our store;
including these below...

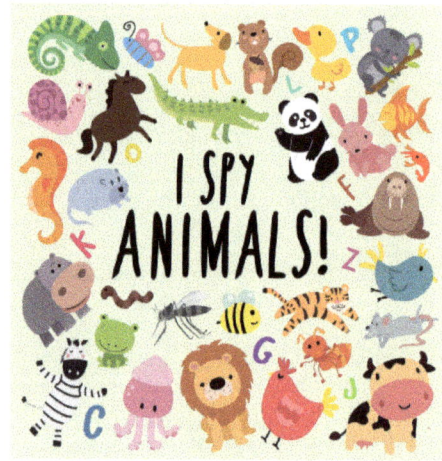

www.ingramcontent.com/pod-product-compliance
Lightning Source LLC
Chambersburg PA
CBHW051249110526
44588CB00025B/2935